Extraordinary Living:
A Life Style Worth Pursuing

Discover the Five Pillars of Support

Richard Goredema

WestBow
PRESS
A DIVISION OF THOMAS NELSON

WestBow Press books may be ordered through booksellers or by contacting:

WestBow Press
A Division of Thomas Nelson
1663 Liberty Drive
Bloomington, IN 47403
www.westbowpress.com
1-(866) 928-1240

Please note: All scripture extractions are from the KING JAMES VERSION (KJV) of the Holy Bible, unless otherwise indicated.

Contact Info: richardgoredema@yahoo.com

ISBN: 978-1-4497-1059-0 (sc)
ISBN: 978-1-4497-1060-6 (e)

Library of Congress Control Number: 2010943069

Printed in the United States of America

WestBow Press rev. date: 1/25/2011

This book equips the readers for the next levels of their influence, to impact the society and make life worth living for themselves and everybody around them. I dedicate this book to people who are yearning for a positive move in life.

<u>Group discussion topics</u> are enlisted after each pillar in this book. These serve as guidelines only, more subjects raised in this book can be explored during your meetings.

SPECIAL THANKS

I thank my wife Theresa who encouraged me to put these thoughts into a book and helped me in editing it too and my daughter Tess-Naishe who endured the less attention she got during the writing of this book.

Lastly my late grandparents, Pastor Peter and Emily Chimheno (Assemblies of God).They introduced the Lord Jesus Christ into my life. The greatest valuable and timeless inheritance one can leave behind for one's loved ones. May the spreading of the good news of Jesus Christ to all generations by any form of medium continue until The Lord Jesus comes back for the church.

CONTENTS

INTRODUCTION

The mind is a sophisticated part of the human being. Besides using our minds to do the things we do, such as thinking and reasoning. The mind has the ability to take you (the person) to places and ages (times) your being has never been before. It can catapult you to the past and the **future**, in such a way that can amaze you, and fall in the danger of dismissing it (what it can do) as a dream which cannot come true. It is a weapon that can destroy or build you and those within your influence. No wonder why the devil is always after it in order to deceive you. So it's vital that you keep it busy with the **things that are GODLY**.PHILLIPIANS 4vs8:FINALLY,BRETHREN, WHATSOEVER THINGS ARE TRUE,WHATSOEVER THINGS ARE HONEST,WHATSOEVER THINGS ARE JUST,WHATSOEVER THINGS ARE PURE,WHATSOEVER THINGS ARE LOVELY,WHATSOEVER THINGS ARE OF A GOOD REPORT;IF THERE BE ANY VIRTUE,AND IF THERE BE ANY PRAISE,THINK ON THESE THINGS.

The question now becomes, what are those thoughts that are GODLY? The desire to get answers to this question is what leads to the compilation of this book. Therefore this book is divided into the following five parts or pillars.

1-The power of the calling

2-To grow is to change

3-Trusting GOD

4-The ability in you

5- Much fruit.

The Apostle Paul said "it's no longer I who lives, but Christ who lives in me". Here is a man whose life had been transformed and taken over by his real purpose of being here on earth. The lifestyle he was now leading was centred on Christ. For instance GOD controlled his spiritual life, his professional life, his socio-economic life and his physical being. In other words GOD called him and he (Paul) understood the calling on his life and he got in line with it by allowing his thoughts to be in line with GOD'S purpose for him. He stands today as one of the people who were very fruitful in their lives here on earth .His fruitfulness has had a very positive impact to this day and age, we study and learn a lot from the letters he wrote to different churches and individuals in the bible.

"If you get your thinking right, you unlock the doors to the treasures GOD has for you, and those after you."

"IF YOU ARE GOING TO MEET AS A GROUP FOR DISCUSSIONS, I RECOMMEND THAT YOU MEET ONCE PER WEEK AND CONCETRATE ON ONE PILLAR PER EACH MEETING."

FIRST PILLAR:
THE POWER OF CALLING

Chapter One: The Reason

There is a relationship between the caller and the called in every aspect of life, no matter how you look at it. When one calls someone either on the phone or across the room or playing field, the caller expects a response from the called. The response may come in different ways. The most common ones are the following (1)The called , does what's desired by the caller.(2) The called ,ignores the caller and continues doing what he/she is doing. (3)The called, delays to do what is required by the caller.(4)The called ,response back and negotiate with the caller.(5)The called ,refuses outright to do what is required of him/her.

"So the way you respond to the caller has a direct impact on your relationship with the one who calls you".

Whether you choose to either ignore or do what you are asked to or delay or refuse, all this has a bearing on your future relationship with person who called(communicated with) you in the first place. So it is important to have our communication channels especially with GOD clear all the time in order to hear what he says or said to us and about us.

The bible tells us that GOD in the beginning created all things .GENESIS 1vs3: AND GOD SAID, LET THERE BE LIGHT: AND THERE WAS LIGHT. In other words the light was called by GOD to be in existence, it surely responded to his calling by coming forth ,as GOD commanded, so was the earth and all creatures, plants and everything in it. It is GOD'S character to call and creation's duty to respond to him as he asks. GOD calls something (someone) with a unique specific purpose according to his master plan. GOD does not nag you, he is not like men who call you, sometimes just to waste your time by either chit chatting or telling you something that does not concern you at all or to spread some rumours about this and that .**"GOD calls with a wholesome purpose to benefit you and his creation at large, do not take his communication with you lightly"**

There are two types of callings that are significant in any creatures existence here on earth. These are (1) IDENTITY, (2) ASSIGNMENT.

Chapter Two: The identity

Lets start by discussing the first one, the GOD given identity. GENESIS 1vs 5: AND GOD CALLED THE LIGHT DAY, AND THE DARKNESS HE CALLED NIGHT.AND THE EVENING AND THE MORNING WERE THE FIRST DAY. When GOD created light he gave it an identity, a name, a character if you like, so did he with darkness. Right up to this generation these identities stand, that's how light and darkness are known –day and night respectively. After creating all creatures GOD gave the responsibility of giving identity to them (creatures) to mankind. GENESIS 2vs 19-20a: AND OUT OF THE GROUND THE LORD GOD FORMED EVERY BEAST OF THE FIELD, AND EVERY FOWL OF THE AIR; AND BROUGHT THEM UNTO ADAM TO SEE WHAT HE WOULD CALL THEM: AND WHATSOEVER ADAM CALLED EVERY LIVING CREATURE, THAT WAS THE NAME THEREOF. AND ADAM GAVE NAMES TO ALL CATTLE, AND TO THE FOWL OF THE AIR, AND TO EVERY BEAST OF THE FIELD...... Whatever Adam gave a name to, so was its identity. For example, a bird with long wings was called an eagle, a tree with very thin leaves was called a pine tree, and a big animal with a trunk was named an elephant and so on. Everything was given a family to belong to, an identity. Mankind's identity is unique in that he is a reflection of the creator himself. GENESIS 1vs 27: SO GOD CREATED MAN IN HIS OWN IMAGE, IN THE IMAGE OF GOD CREATED HE HIM; MALE AND FEMALE CREATED HE THEM. Humankinds' identity is that of GOD himself. We are an image of GOD. In other words GOD passed his characteristics to us. He created (called out) man and gave him an identity (image) that is his. That is why GOD passed on the responsibility of naming (calling) all the other creatures, to humankind. Therefore as humankind our identity is GODLY. Because of that ability in us, we as humans are able to name ourselves into different families, tribes and languages, this ability is a GODLY character, and it brings forth his glory in diversity.

"Everything ever created has a name, a family, it is identified with". But humankind has somewhat belittled this, for example in some parts of the world, mankind has sought identity in animals such as lions, fish, eagles, elephants, cows, and so forth. This is also very common in sporting activities, you hear of a sport team calling itself the Lions, the Swallows, the Sharks and so on. Mankind seeks to identify with these creatures' attributes so much that undeserving relevance and exaltation is given to these creatures, above all other things including him: this is wrong.

In the bible we hear of references to animals in relation to mankind as well, but in a right way. ISAIAH 40vs31: BUT THEY THAT WAIT UPON THE LORD SHALL RENEW THEIR STRENGH; THEY SHALL MOUNT UP WITH WINGS AS EAGLES; THEY SHALL RUN, AND NOT BE WEARY; AND THEY SHALL WALK, AND NOT FAINT. The eagle is given as reference to mankind because of its resilience among other things. PROVERBS 6vs 6: GO TO THE ANT, THOU SLUGGARD; CONSIDER HER WAYS, AND BE WISE. This is an insect known for its industriousness and foresight, something mankind should emulate not revere. JOHN 1vs29: THE NEXT DAY JOHN SEETH JESUS COMING UNTO HIM, AND SAITH, BEHOLD THE LAMB OF GOD, WHICH TAKETH AWAY THE SIN OF THE WORLD. The Lord Jesus Christ is referred to as the lamp because this animal was being offered as a sacrifice during the Passover. Jesus Christ was offered as a sacrifice to take away the sins of the world by GOD the father. Biblical references such as these help us to develop a deeper revelation and understanding of the love and care and abilities GOD has invested in us, should we observe these creatures we learn something to our benefit.

Therefore it is okay to appreciate the creatures' abilities which are beyond our abilities for as long as we do it to learn some lessons about how we should conduct ourselves with others and see the glory of GOD in them, thanking him for creating these for us. We must always remember that mankind is the image of GOD, (not eagles, ants, cows etc) and there is nothing more superior to humans here on earth.

Chapter Three: The Assignment

GOD has given mankind an assignment here on earth. Each one of us has his/her assignment or job or better still a calling to fulfil before departing this planet .This calling is not man arranged but it is man related, in other words your assignment was delivered and mandated to you by your creator and in order to fulfil it, you have to use what your creator put inside you together with what surrounds you here on earth.

Let's look at our Lord Jesus Christ. Our father GOD gave him an assignment to deliver the world from bondage of the devil. LUKE 4vs18-19:THE SPIRIT OF THE LORD IS UPON ME,BECAUSE HE HATH ANOINTED ME TO PREACH THE GOSPEL TO THE POOR;HE HATH SENT ME TO HEAL THE BROKENHEARTED,TO PREACH DELIVERANCE TO THE CAPTIVES,AND RECOVERY OF SIGHT TO THE BLIND,TO SET AT LIBERTY THEM THAT ARE BRUISED,TO PREACH THE ACCEPTABLE YEAR OF THE LORD. When Jesus came he was given an identity, a name, Emmanuel (GOD with us).MATTHEW 1vs23: BEHOLD, A VIRGIN SHALL BE WITH CHILD, AND SHALL BRING FORTH A SON, AND THEY SHALL CALL HIS NAME EMMANUEL, AND WHICH BEING INTERPRETED GOD WITH US. Thus he was called, and he belonged to a family, which literally means he could now be identified with life on earth, even though he was the son of GOD. Meaning where Joseph and Mary went he also went, what they ate, he also ate, who they associated with, he also did, and their culture became his culture. Furthermore GOD gave him an assignment, a calling upon his life, his mission, his purpose, **his calling**, which he articulately accomplished on the cross. In between, during his course of life; Jesus had a career, some trade training if you like. Joseph his earthly father being a carpenter trained Jesus the skills of the trade so, during his life before turning 30 years, he would help occasionally in the workshop. His earthly family identity and skills training (career) did not stop him from fulfilling his assignment (calling). Rather he used all this to his advantage and preached the good news. By being called Joseph's son, Jesus was accepted as any human being and by practising carpentry he proved that he was not lazy and can earn a living just like anybody else that has a career. So many a time in this generation, mankind tend to be confused or undecided or be ignorant about which is which as far as a career and a calling over their lives is concerned. I believe that according to GOD'S order of importance, a calling upon your life is more important than your career.

"Your career must support your calling, not vice versa". Your career can be changed but your calling cannot, your career is mostly for your personal benefit whereas your calling benefits GOD'S creation at large, humans, animals, nature and so on it goes to meet far beyond your personal needs and wants. When a person is born, GOD wraps inside that person talents and gifts, these form the foundation of what that person is going to be and to do in life. These talents and gifts can be recognised from an early age by that particular person and also by the other people around him or her. For instance some people have great voices that can sing others are very eloquent they can give speeches that have substance, others athletic and others smart, intelligent and others just submissive they are at their best when working under somebody or under instruction. We all have packages that areGOD given in each one of us. All it takes is just for us to discover what's in these packages and how we can use the contents. The diagram below will help illustrate the above:

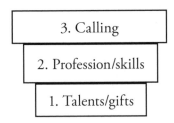

1-Talents/gifts: These are GOD given, our foundation to build our lives on.

2-Profession/skills: These we are trained to do, at colleges, universities etc, these trainings humble us, refine us and sharpen us. This is where we get to be mentored and imparted whether it's through a bible school, business school, medical school, arts school, law school etc .Careers can be changed for example a lawyer can change to be a lecturer, a teacher to be a politician, a footballer to be a businessperson.

3-Calling: This is GOD given, it is the pinnacle of life, your purpose, and your destiny .It must be complimented by your talents and career. You need GOD'S anointing for this, whether you are a businessperson, social worker or administrator. LUKE 4vs 18: THE SPIRIT OF THE LORD IS UPON ME, BECAUSE HE HATH ANOINTED ME TO PREACH THE GOSPEL TO THE POOR, HE HATH SENT ME TO HEAL THE BROKENHEARTED, TO PREACH DELIVERANCE TO THE CAPTIVES, AND RECOVERY OF SIGHT TO THE BLIND, TO SET AT LIBERTY THEM THAT ARE BRUISED.GOD anoints people who do what he created them to do. He empowers, he equips and he gives favour both with man and himself, to such people. Your calling cannot be changed, you can only discover more of your potential (what you can do) by the revelation from GOD.

Reference to the diagram:

With (1) you can do this much.

With (2) you can do that much.

With (3) you can do much more.

By obeying GOD'S calling upon your life, you place yourself in a position of pouring out every ability GOD has put in you, for the world to see and benefit. You leave an impact which no one can erase. People will read about you, hear about you, study and use your works. All in all mankind will see the goodness of GOD through you.

I was watching a television talk show another day, the hostess had a business executive as the guest .The guest was sharing his belief that he had finally found his calling. The man narrated his story saying, he went on holiday from the USA to the Far East Asia, and there he stabled into a community which lived in abject poverty and it touched him most was that the children there were not attending school, simply because there were no schools in the community. So when he went back to the USA, he took it upon himself to do something about this situation. The man used his influence, his network of associates, his financial resources, His stored away treasure, his skills to start building a school for that community in the Far East. To date he has built numerous schools in that part of the world. He has given up his executive status at his company, what he does fulltime is helping bring education to the under privileged and he does not regret it. Thousands are getting educated because of his works.

"Blessed are you, if you can use your talent/gift, training, education and anointing at the same time to achieve one goal."

GOD does not force us to do anything, even if it's good for us. He has given to mankind a free will. He reveals to us what he wants done and simply expects us to cooperate with him. Providing all the resources for the assignments and we get the job done. So it is squarely upon us to accept his calling on our lives or to reject, ignore or postpone it. So what happens when we reject his assignment and what also happens when we accept it? See book of JONAH 1vs1-17; in chapter one of this book we meet Jonah who was a prophet of GOD, diverting or running away from an assignment GOD had given him, to go to Nineveh. He instead boarded a Tashish bound ship, thus rejecting GOD'S plan for him. Therefore let's discuss what happens when one rejects GOD'S assignment.

1-Your rejection of GOD'S assignment affects not only you, but others also, in a very negative way. The people who were with Jonah in the ship to Tashish lost their belongings during the storm; they threw their goods into the sea, trying to lighten the load of the ship. So by rejecting GOD'S calling and tasks you bring loses instead of profits into peoples' lives, instead of progress, people around you or in your company retrogress.

2- You bring confusion around you. People were confused by the behaviour of the sea, they just did not know what to do, they really never expected such weather conditions to prevail, and it looked like it was not the season for such storms so they were caught unawares. People will always be caught off guard by events or happenings that will have an adverse effect on their lives.

3-Rejecting GOD'S assignment will have you living with guilt and fear and spreading this to other people as well, there is no peace and tranquillity around you. Therefore look around you: your family, your workplace your community, your church, observe all the "not so good things "could you be the reason why those things are happening simply because you are rejecting the calling of GOD upon your life?

JONAH 3vs1-10; should you choose to accept GOD'S assignment for your life, what then happened with Jonah when he accepted, is going to happen with you and your community.

1-People of Nineveh <u>believed </u>the Lord, the GOD Jonah served instead of other gods.

2-People of Nineveh <u>obeyed </u>the word of GOD; they fasted, humbling themselves before him.

3-People of Nineveh <u>repented </u>from their sins and were saved, that happened to be the main task Jonah went there for. GOD'S grace was abounding over mankind in this city.

4-Jonah's message was heard by the king of this city:

"Should you accept and do GOD'S assignment in your life, GOD guarantees favour and authority be it in your family, workplace, country or community and even in political circles."

The will of the lord prevails when we accept and do the work GOD called us to do. (Nineveh was saved).

Chapter Four: Hindrances to the calling

When GOD'S calling is upon your life a lot of elements come throwing themselves at you some good and some bad. The bad ones can be identified as hindrances. Now there are different hindrances that seek to stop us from fulfilling what GOD the father has equipped us to do. Some of these are:

1-THE DEVIL'S INTERCEPTION, when you start doing something for GOD and somewhere in the process an event or happening takes place and forces you to put your plans about the work of GOD at hand aside for a while.

2-DIVERSION, this is when something not related to your assignment comes in and takes centre stage at the expense of the assignment GOD has given you.

3-PROCRASTINATION, this is when you postpone your assignment for another day, time or even another year.

4-DEPRESSION,this is when other issues about your life affect you negatively so much that you lack the zeal to do anything with enthusiasm ,including answering to GOD'S call on your life.

5-DOUBT, when you lack the faith needed to accomplish what GOD wants you to accomplish. You are not so sure if this is GOD or not. This is also caused by fear.

6-LOW SELF-ESTEEM, this is when you look at yourself ,your family background ,your education and material and spiritual achievements and conclude that they are not good enough for what GOD wants you to do. This is very effective when you compare yourself with others whom you think are better than you, and seem to be suitable for the job.

7-INTEMIDATION, this is when achievements of others seem to overshadow what you can achieve. You look at your work versus other peoples' work and conclude that your work is insignificant therefore not worth pursuing at all.

8-LONELINESS, this is when you feel you have no support or partners to do your work. In such cases there seem to be no back-up service in your assignment. In some instances the devil blinds you so much that you won't see the resources at your disposal ,all you see is your inabilities and limits and this will cause you to abandon ship,1 KINGS 19 vs. 9-10:AND HE CAME THITHER UNTO A CAVE,AND LODGED THERE,AND ,BEHOLD THE WORD OF THE LORD CAME TO HIM,AND HE SAID UNTO HIM,WHAT DOEST THOU HERE,ELIJAH?.AND HE SAID ,I HAVE BEEN VERY JEALOUS FOR THE LORD GOD OF HOSTS;FOR THE CHILDREN OF ISRAEL HAVE FORSAKEN THY COVENANT,AND THOWN DOWN THINE ALTARS,AND SLAIN THY PROPHETS WITH THE SWORD ;AND I EVEN I ONLY,AM LEFT;AND THEY SEEK MY LIFE,TO TAKE IT AWAY. The prophet of GOD ,Elijah is so overwhelmed by the opposition that his previous successes are wiped off his mind and all he thinks of is his adversary and even the thought of the ability and potential of GOD to back him does not cross his mind .God had to intervene and strengthen him because there was still a lot be done by him (not anyone else).1 KINGS 19 vs18 :YET I HAVE LEFT ME SEVEN THOUSAND IN ISRAEL,ALL THE KNEES WHICH HAVE NOT BOWED UNTO BAAL,AND EVERY MOUTH WHICH HATH NOT KISSED HIM. GOD reveals to him that there are still more like him who are obedient and can answer to GOD'S call upon their lives. I am sure this was a morale booster for Elijah.

"Whatever hindrances that may come our way, when we are doing what GOD has called us to do, GOD who started the good_work in us will finish it, he is the beginning and the end. Let's_follow his instructions concerning the challenges at hand".

There are ways or answers to dealing with what the devil throws at us when we really set ourselves for the calling GOD has for us. Our thought lives must be harnessed with the things of GOD. Normally what we think is what we end up doing, which is in order to be doing good we need to have good thoughts. PHILIPPIANS 2vs5: LET THIS MIND BE IN YOU, WHICH WAS ALSO IN CHRIST. Apostle Paul looks at the life of Christ and concludes that it is because of what he thought that made him to do what he did and these deeds made him to accomplish his mission and purpose on earth. MATTHEW 4vs3-4:AND WHEN THE TEMPTER CAME TO HIM,HE SAID,IF THOU BE THE SON OF GOD,COMMAND THAT THESE STONES BE MADE BREAD,BUT HE ANSWERED AND SAID ,IT IS WRITTEN ,MAN SHALL NOT LIVE BY BREAD ALONE ,BUT BY EVERY WORD THAT PROCEEDETH OUT OF THE MOUTH OF GOD. In this chapter our Lord Jesus Christ shows us the most powerful weapon the devil cannot withstand; the word of GOD. Jesus shows us how it's done and does it in the process .As people with a GODLY mission we need to fill ourselves with the word of GOD, it's a weapon to crush any opposition from the devil. The devil tried to make Jesus abandon the mission or assignment or his calling, and he failed simply because Jesus was full of nothing but the word, he countered what the devil was saying with what was in his mind, the word of GOD, rightfully using and explaining it to his enemy (please note) not distorting it and confusing himself like the devil did.

How then do we saturate ourselves with the word? For us to have the word we need to read and study the bible and seek understanding by the help of the Holy Spirit. For us to read and study the word, we need to set aside time for it, and in order to set aside time for it we need to organise ourselves well and prioritise our daily activities.

"That which is of paramount importance to you, ranks high in your priorities".

NEHEMIAH CHAPTERS 1-6:

Nehemiah is one good example of a person who gave himself to GOD and GOD showed himself to Israel through him. The rebuilding of the wall of Jerusalem was a mammoth task, it needed divine intervention. During the process hindrances sprouted out, but Nehemiah pressed forward and ultimately what was once his vision became a reality. Working together with a team, they used their gifts, talents and education, work experience or career skills to do what GOD called them to do, their assignment.

Whatever God has called you to do ,whether it's to invent ,to preach, to sing, business leadership or charity work go for it all systems firing.

<u>**GROUP DISCUSSIONS:**</u>

-Can you share with others what you believe is your "calling" and explain why you think so, if possible give a practical example of the work you have been involved in.

-What challenges are you facing right now in your pursuit of the will of GOD upon your life, and are your talents and skills supplementing your calling.

Notes

_____

_____

_____

_____

_____

_____

_____

_____

_____

_____

_____

_____

_____

_____

_____

SECOND PILLAR
TO GROW IS TO CHANGE

Chapter Five: The process of Growth

I remember vividly well when I was a kid, that when at school my teacher would always ask this question;

"What do you want to be when you grow up"? Various answers would come up from my peers and me .These included, a policeman, teacher, doctor, nurse, truck driver, and lawyer and so on. I don't remember anyone of us saying he/she wants to be nobody or wants to do nothing.

What we did understand then about growth was that one day I will be a man/woman and stop being a girl/boy and take care of myself instead of my parents doing it for me. What we did not comprehend though was the fact that **growing up is a process of change**, change which had to occur not only physically but mentally, materially, professionally, socially and even spiritually.

The bible says GOD gives seed to the sower. It is this seed which I want in this context to refer to as the foundation of growth. When a seed is in your hand, it's meant to be transferred to the ground; in order for it to be relevant to creation, otherwise besides that it amounts to nothing. So growth comes from a seed thought, a nucleus, small but big when we start acting on it. Therefore what we think in our minds is seed which we must then put into action in order for it to grow and consequently give us life. This then represents a process of change from one stage to another. JOHN 10vs10: THE THIEF COMETH NOT, BUT FOR TO STEAL, AND TO KILL AND TO DESTROY: I AM COME THAT THEY MIGHT HAVE LIFE, AND THAT THEY MIGHT HAVE IT MORE

ABUNTANTLY. The reason for growth is that we should live tomorrow and not only for tomorrow but to prepare life for future generations as well and this life includes spirituality as well. In other words where there is no thought of tomorrow, there is no seed and where there is no seed, there is no growth and **where there is no growth** there **is death.**

JOHN 14vs2: IN MY FATHER'S HOUSE ARE MANY MANSIONS: IF IT WERE NOT SO, I WOULD HAVE TOLD YOU . I GO TO PREPARE A PLACE FOR YOU. When Jesus ascended to heaven, he went to continue the process of growth in heaven. Emphasising the fact that he came to give us life in abundance. The bible tells us that he is busy preparing a place for us, where the streets are of gold and death has no place there. As we live here on earth right now, there is some massive construction going on in heaven, some growth is taking place ,mansions are being built, a reception for the bride (the church) of Jesus Christ is being prepared, some facelifts are taking place, decorations being done, its massive, something our minds cannot comprehend. Change is taking place; there is life up there, glory to GOD!

In our natural world, growth is stimulated by several habits or actions. Let's discuss the human body: it needs to be on a balanced diet, thus what you eat must contribute to a good start of growth which is not prone to diseases and illnesses. We need to put our physical bodies on a schedule of exercise for them to remain strong and carry us through life and of course we need oxygen to survive. As for our mission here on earth, we need to have what I call "a balanced state of mind", and it is stimulated by our spiritual, physical, socio-economic activities we engage in. Without these our growth in whatever area of life, be it in business or life in general is hampered. What then happens if we are found wanting in our "state of mind"? When we don't seem to balance our spiritual, physical, socio economic lives in order to grow wholesomely, and at the same time our communities and families are pinning high hopes of change from us, we ourselves not worried much about it because we feel it's not yet our time to make a move. This is when expectations are high for us to deliver then there is something we can learn from the fig tree mentioned below.

MARK 11vs12-13: AND ON THE MORROW ,WHEN THEY WERE FROM BETHANY,HE WAS HUNGRY:AND AFTER SEEING A FIG TREE AFAR OFF HAVING LEAVES HE CAME,IF HAPLY HE MIGHT FIND ANYTHING THEREON:AND WHEN HE CAME

TO IT,HE FOUND NOTHING BUT LEAVES ;FOR THE TIME OF FIGS WAS NOT YET. In this text the Lord Jesus saw a fig tree; being hungry he was expecting to eat the fruit of this tree. In his mind the hunger issue was now solved an answer to it had been found. His hopes were high but alas it was not so, because the fig tree was not in the season of bearing fruit and there was nothing wrong with that, it was ok for it to be in the state it was in and even the disciples who were with Jesus saw nothing wrong with the fig tree at this time of the year. But this was not so with Jesus, the state of the fig tree was not pleasing at all. Jesus knew the potential of this fig tree, he knew its purpose, that of bearing figs. He was in other words expecting to see change in the form of bearing figs. He was expecting growth regardless of the circumstances; GOD the father put the seed of growth in this fig tree so that ultimately it may bring forth life. In this particular time it was not bearing time but all the same there was someone hoping for fruitfulness and when nothing was found on it, death was bestowed upon it. The same scenario is common in mankind, we are expected to grow and produce in all areas of our lives, spiritually, professionally, socio-economically and even physically and so on. For as long as the thought is there ,the seed of growth is in the hand regardless of the circumstances or seasons we are in. Our Lord is hoping we do the impossible in the eyes of the world, which is to initiate growth in the face of adversity. Bring change when it is least expected. We may need to ask ourselves the following questions as individuals and be as honest with ourselves as possible:

1-What is it that GOD has put in me?

2-Is it waiting for the right time (season) to come out?

3-If so when is the right time/season?

Must we put aside the issue of expansion or growth and change until when all things are going on for us, when we have all the cards on the table? I believe the answer is a big NO.2 TIMOTHY 4vs2: PREACH THE WORD; BE INSTANT IN SEASON, OUT OF SEASON; REPROVE, REBUKE, EXHORT WITH ALL LONGSUFFERING AND DOCTRINE. Paul admonishes Timothy to preach the word in all seasons: when it's conducive to do so and not conducive to do so. A season is a time span set for something expected, to happen. And when it happens within that particular season, people see and take it as a normal and natural happening within that time span. Should an event or something happen when it is least expected and most cases no preparation for it has been done, then that catches people unawares and in most cases surprises them. So Paul is telling Timothy to disregard peoples' expectations when it comes to preaching the gospel. He is telling him to remain thinking, speaking and acting according to the word of GOD, in spite of what surrounds him at the time. In other words Timothy is encouraged to propel growth (preaching) regardless of the circumstances prevailing at the time.

"Therefore it is not the season /time that brings forth growth/change in our lives but what we do in that particular season we are in; is what makes the difference".

Our actions can and will bring growth to our activities even if our geographical location ,economical state ,family backgrounds, educational knowledge and even race put us at a disadvantage. All we need to do is PREACH (think about growth, speak about growth, act on growth).

Some few years ago we had a funeral in the family .An aunt of mine went to be with the Lord. During the funeral service her pastor and several brethren she fellowshipped with, said something that caught my attention, they gave an account of how she laboured in the lord at the local church. She was the church choir leader, member of the church womens' committee and very active in the church's welfare activities .What got my attention most was that she had the zeal to do all this work in spite of the challenges which I knew were before her .She did not have the standard of education which would qualify someone for such responsibilities. Her source of income was not something one can envy. In spite of all this she had the boldness to preach and encourage other women, some of them very educated and with stable jobs. She propelled growth in what GOD called her to do, overlooking all the setbacks that were before her.

"We must overcome pessimisms in order for us to grow."

It's what we do, not what we go through that matters most. What are you doing seeing that you are going through what you going through?

Growth is unavoidable to you, as long as you are living. You either flow with it, that is letting circumstances dictate your way and your future, or you show it the way, in other words grabbing the steering wheel of your bus and driving it. Let me present to you the 2 options mentioned above:

Option 1-Should you choose to flow with it, that is simply taking a back seat and letting things that have an indirect or direct impact in your life take their course without your GOD given authority. The probability of underperforming and not reaching your potential is very high. Let's refer again to the fig tree. There was nothing questionable really about the health of this tree. It was growing at a pace it should have been, letting the forces of nature directing its flow. The tree was producing fruits when it was time for fruits, shedding leaves when it is time to do so, everything flowing smoothly. But when circumstances took a different turn, the unexpected became the expected. When it was confronted with a situation where it had to dig deep into its potential to serve and survive, it was found wanting. What happened as a result of its shortcomings is for us to learn from, it died.

Let us come close to home; the story of a fig tree will be illustrated as this, John was an entrepreneur, he operated an office equipment retail business. It specialised in sourcing products such as chairs, desks, computers and stationery for the local business community. This man had a vision for his business which was well supported by his customers, his bankers and his staff. The economy of the country in which he lived was quiet sound, In order to purchase his products from abroad he only needed to talk to his bankers to organise the finances for him in foreign exchange rates. The companies he supplied to would pay him as per their agreements. His staff would get incentives for their performances on top of their wages .Even being a small and upcoming company as it was, he could afford to give loans to his staff members whenever they needed them and this kept them motivated as a team and the future was as bright as the sun. He was planning to expand the company to other regions of the country. Then suddenly factors which were beyond their control started to affect his promising business and these included Politics: the government of his country was getting isolated by its friends because of some of its policies, Economy: because of the isolation, investors were pulling out, few international organisations wanted to partner with the locals and this meant little money coming into the country to keep the economy running. Factors such as drought spared nothing on the agricultural side. Consequently his bankers could not afford to operate on the same terms as before. His customers began to scale down on purchases because they were retrenching workers.

John was left with just one choice; to slow down and ultimately close shop. The vision died killed by circumstances. This is what **negative growth** ultimately produces.

Option 2-Should you choose to grab the bull by the horns this scripture will strengthen you: DEUTERONOMY 28vs13: AND THE LORD SHALL MAKE THEE THE HEAD, AND NOT THE TAIL; AND THOU SHALT BE ABOVE ONLY, AND THOU SHALT NOT BE BENEATH; IF THAT THOU HEARKEN UNTO THE COMMANDMENTS OF THE LORD THY GOD, WHICH I COMMAND THEE THIS DAY, TO OBSERVE AND TO DO THEM. The bible reveals the promises to you and me; the children of GOD.As you seek to take charge of events in your life that pertain to your progress in life, know this; you must be the head not the tail. In other words you must be the "brains" behind everything that happens in your life –process. Put your brains to work, think ahead, strategize, and be proactive not reactive; always seek to be "streets ahead" of the pack, desire to know what the future holds for your career, family, etc through answers from the word of GOD .Also desire knowledge and wisdom and seek it. Plan and implement the plans.

"Discipline yourself on matters concerning your flesh and finances".

The reverse is true if you allow yourself to be the "tail". The tail is "brainless", that is it does not think, plan, see, hear, taste, smell and is always on the back, never in the front. Literally meaning its "life" is run and controlled by other members of the body, it knows nothing about what lies ahead and what's following behind. What a miserable life to live if you are a tail.

If you are to initiate growth you need to think out of the box, think and reason differently, push a little more. Have you ever imagined what was going on in the minds of the people who have invented some of the world famous gadgets we use today? Imagine what got into the mind of the gentlemen who invented the automobile, the aeroplane, the television, the telephone, etc. I am told the man who invented the light bulb did not get it right easily. He "failed" several times and these failures did not deter him from his vision, instead he accepted them positively and took them as other formulas he discovered which cannot produce a light bulb and not as failures per say.

"A positive attitude is fundamental in pursuit of growth".

The same principle applies to people who seek to lose weight. The day they embark on a programme to lose excess weight, one will be fired-up, working and sticking to the advice at hand, always weighing oneself on the scale to check whether those undesired kilos/pounds are burning away I am told during the initial stages the kilos do burn in very large proportions which is very encouraging. But as the day /weeks/ months go by, your percentage loss gets smaller and smaller and this can be discouraging and may tempt the candidate to give up the programme midway, before attaining the right weight.

PROVERBS 23vs7:FOR AS HE THINKETH IN HIS HEART ,SO IS HE....You are what you think of yourself on issues concerning your careers, relations health, family, relationship with GOD and your future in general. If it's in your mind; you can achieve it. HOSEA 4vs6: MY PEOPLE ARE DISTROYED FOR LACK OF KNOWLEDGE: BECAUSE THOU HAST REJECTED KNOWLEDGE, I WILL ALSO REJECT THEE, THAT THOU SHALT BE NO PRIEST TO ME: SEEING THOU HAST FORGOTTEN THE LAW OF THY GOD, I WILL ALSO FORGET THY CHILDREN. This scripture talks about why we as people perish: lack of knowledge. Without knowing where we are going in life or not liking the path our lives are leading us to, we won't see the purpose why we are here on earth and this cripples growth and ultimately we die, professionally, spiritually, mentally and even physically. Seeing and knowing where you are going indicates the potential of change. You can initiate even in the face of adversity. So are you leading somewhere or you are being led somewhere?

Chapter Six: Road maps of Growth

There are several avenues one can follow or take in order to initiate and propel growth. In whatever you are involved in, it could be your day to day activities at work, college, home, church or in your community .Please note that much of the issues under this topic are dealt with in the "Much Fruit" pillar later in the book.

1-Desire to ADD A NEW DIMENSION IN YOUR TASK; Always analyse and see if you cannot flavour things a bit, just for the fun of it, if not for anything else. Tell me who on earth does not want a dose of fun, even if the task at hand calls for seriousness and deep thinking. A little bit of fun eases tensions and refreshes ideas.

2-There are certain tasks that come our ways, that are too heavy to bear, such situations are very common among families. Should you find yourself in that situation, seek to BE THE ONE WHO LIGHTENS THE BURDEN.A death or sickness in the family for example can be a devastating, depressing and challenging event to come to terms with. Such a happening can leave the brothers, sisters, parents, aunts, uncles, cousins and family friends dejected, disoriented, bitter, hopeless and sometimes clueless. What do you do in such a situation? You must help in carrying the burden, where there is need for finance to settle bills for example, contribute not because you have surplus but because you want to make life easier for others. For the same reason participate in the crisis that might involve transportation, shelter, food, education, etc.

3-God has given to each human being some gifts and talents. These are not just for ourselves but for the benefit of others we live with, at work places colleges, communities, country and the whole world at large. So in the event of your absence it must be felt by everybody that life is not as enjoyable as it must be. Therefore through your gift or talent, BE THE MISSING PART OF THE PUZZLE OF LIFE, if you are absent from your folks. How would it feel to wake up one day and find that your best friend is no more? Or your favourite TV show has been struck off air indefinitely? Or your spiritual leader has decided to change cities or countries for that matter? Happenings such as these kind of put your life on hold a bit, don't they? In the case of a friend you are bound to miss companionship, secrets sharing, laughter, jokes ,dreams sharing, opinions and just words of wisdom to make life decisions, The same applies for the TV show, and the spiritual leader. Therefore use your gifts and talents not for yourself only, but for that fellow human being GOD has blessed you to be in contact with, whilst you are still together.

4-God has put you where you are right now for a good reason. You are suppose to be doing whatever you are doing in order to improve the situation that surrounds you, in a GODLY manner. Remember that before you, there was someone wearing those shoes, doing your job/task. Your paramount duty now is to TAKE IT FROM YOUR PREDESSESOR AND IMPROVE ON IT. It could be a ministry, business, job responsibilities or simply an intelligent idea on paper yet to be implemented .Ask yourself. "How can I take this responsibility I have a notch higher than it is right now"?Can you imagine that not so long ago we used to have telephones only and now we have both the telephone and different types of cell phones ,an improvement of the former.

Chapter Seven: Examples and Factors of Growth

Let's look at some of the people who did phenomenal things that are recorded down as elements of growth.

1-In the bible for example we have David.1 SAMUEL 17vs15;34-35:BUT DAVID WENTAND RETURNED FROM SAUL TO FEED HIS FATHER'S SHEEP AT BETHLEHEM.AND DAVID SAID UNTO SAUL,THY SERVANT KEPT HIS FATHER'S SHEEP,AND THERE CAME A LION,AND A BEAR,AND TOOK A LAMP OUT OF THE FLOCK AND I WENT AFTER HIM,AND SMOTE HIM,AND DELIVERED IT OUT OF HIS MOUTH:AND WHEN HE AROSE AGAINST ME,I CAUGHT HIM BY HIS BEARD,AND SMOTE HIM,AND SLEW HIM. The above scripture confirm that David was a shepherd boy. His primary business was to keep and protect his father's sheep. He would spend all his day out in the fields with the sheep.1SAMUEL 18vs5; 13: AND DAVID WENT OUT WHITHERSOEVER SAUL SENT HIM, AND BEHAVED WISELY: AND SAUL SET HIM OVER THE MEN OF WAR, AND HE WAS ACCEPTED IN THE SIGHT OF ALL PEOPLE, AND ALSO IN THE SIGHT OF SAUL'S SERVANTS. THEREFORE SAUL REMOVED HIM FROM HIM, AND MADE HIM HIS CAPTAIN OVER A THOUSAND; AND HE WENT OUT AND CAME IN BEFORE THE PEOPLE. Here David is mentioned as a warrior and a captain of the army; he is no longer in charge of the sheep but soldiers. Therefore David grows or changed from protecting stock to protecting the nation. There is vast differences between the two, some of the differences are:

[1a] People expect to find the following in you; integrity, honesty, efficiency, skill and motivational abilities whereas animals are not fussy about your character or potential.

[1b] GOD has given people the ability to think and reason over issues and matters that arise whereas animals do not do that.

[1c]People can be judgemental and can disagree with your decisions whereas animals simply follow your lead with little or resistance at all.

[1d] People do offer exceptional service back, they are there for you, day and night whereas animals have to be commanded most of the time to serve you and their service has limitations.

[1e] People need security and assurance on matters concerning food, shelter, education, health, peace etc. Whereas animals do not have lifetime plans.

Therefore David had to change his leadership methods from what he had been used to whilst herding sheep in order to progress to the next level towards his destiny in life: that of leading soldiers.

"The methods we use to do our chores today may not be applicable and effective in our next stage in life, as such there is need to evaluate and change them in order for us to grow and be relevant to society".

2-The death of King David did not stop growth. In fact it ushered in a new dimension and dispensation of a growth bearer, in the form of Solomon, his son..

[2a] 1 KINGS 5vs 4;12:BUT NOW THE LORD MY GOD HATH GIVEN ME REST ON EVERY SIDE ,SO THAT THERE IS NEITHER ADVERSARY NOR EVIL OCCURRENT.AND THE LORD GAVE SOLOMON WISDOM, AS HE PROMISED HIM: AND THERE WAS PEACE BETWEEM HIRAM AND SOLOMON ;AND THE TWO MADE A LEAGUE TOGETHER. When Solomon became king, he did things his father had not done even though his father had so wished do to them. In the above verse the bible says Solomon was able to bring peace to

Israel. Israel had seen many wars prior to Solomon .So for the first time in a long period the nation moved from the battlefield to tranquillity.

[2b] I KINGS 4vs34: AND THERE CAME OF ALL PEOPLE TO HEAR THE WISDOM OF SOLOMON, FROM ALL KINGS OF THE EARTH, WHICH HAD HEARD OF HIS WISDOM.GOD gave Solomon wisdom, such that the nation of Israel was transformed from an ordinary small nation to an extraordinary famous nation. This transformation was so remarkable that other kings paid visits to see and hear first hand for themselves, King Solomon's words and deeds.

[2c] 1 KINGS 10vs28-29:AND SOLOMON HAD HORSES BROUGHT OUT OF EGYPT,AND LINEN YARN: THE KING'S MERCHANTS RECEIVED THE LINEN YARN AT A PRICE.AND A CHARIOT CAME UP AND WENT OUT OF EGYPT FOR SIX HUNDRED SHEKELS OF SILVER,AND AN HORSE FOR AN HUNDRED AND FIFTY:AND SO FOR ALL THE KINGS OF THE HITTITES,AND FOR THE KINGS OF SYRIA,DID THEY BRING THEM OUT BY THEIR MEANS.GOD gave king Solomon some business skills which his father David did not have. Solomon was able to turn some of the former enemies of Israel into business associates. Solomon did what probably David wished to do if he were alive by that time.

"The legacy left by our predecessors forms the platform for the basis of growth, and the desire for growth must be the driving force for change."

3-Medical history tells us that the first successful heart surgery was performed by a gentleman called Chris Barnard. We are told that after the operation the patients would stay hospitalised for months whilst medical personnel monitored the progress on day to day basis. But since then there has been some improvement and changes in medical technology and methods, such that in an event of an operation of the heart, the patients can be hospitalised just for days and be left to recover in the comfort of their homes.

4-Other examples of growth take the form of name changes in business and change of company logos etc. I believe changes such as these happen because of the desire to grow or expand. Such changes bring in new dimensions of conducting business, such as new markets. New technology, innovation and ideas that can sustain the enterprise. Change not only attracts the attention of the potential or targeted market, but your competitors also, thereby keeping the economy active for the benefit of the consumer.

For anything to grow in a healthy way an environment that is conducive which suits its characteristics must be created. For example if you are growing flowers commercially you need to know among other things such as water, good soil, insecticides etc, that flowers do need lots of light even in the middle of the night, for them to flourish to the best of their ability. Therefore such an atmosphere must be created if you are serious about a good harvest. The same thing applies even when raising children, if you raise them in a violent environment, violence is all they will know and violence is what they will produce. So as an individual when you seek to grow and change from where you are right now take cognisance of your environment. Find out what is affecting your plans for growth and see if it is for you or against you.

"A good atmosphere for growth must be able to produce a support system for your work, when you need support."

This support system is birthed out of your determination for change and it in cooperates factors that are spiritual, financial, material and educational. You may ask how this support system can come about.

2 TIMOTHY 2vs15: STUDY TO SHEW THYSELF APPROVED UNTO GOD, A WORKMAN THAT NEEDETH NOT TO BE ASHAMED, RIGHTLY DIVIDING THE WORD OF TRUTH. Paul encourages Timothy to study .In other words he tells Timothy to learn from others .So as we seek to grow lets desire knowledge. We must attend seminars, courses, workshops and network with others who are involved in activities of our interest, people whom we can take a leaf out of their books. We must associate with the right people; people who will motivate, encourage, share ideas, and positively critics us. If we have such a support system, then we know we are in good company. If there is a good company, then there must be also a bad company. This is an association which will do among other negative thinks towards us, discourage us. The last thing you need on this path of growth is discouragement. Whenever you sense it, disassociate yourself and seek other friends, companionship or association. Discouragement is like poison, that when it is poured on a plant or food to be consumed, it brings death either instantly or gradually.

Growing is a process not an event. There are choices to be made. Because a lot of opportunities do present themselves to you along the way, you need to be wise enough to know which ones will help you reach your full potential. There are preparations to be done .If you do not prepare for something you want to have, then you are actually preparing for something you do not want, unknowingly. Therefore if you believe in achieving, get ready to achieve. As you grow, you change and as you change, you face challenges or obstacles and these are tests to see if you really mean it. Therefore you cannot really grow until you have been through some tests. During the process of change there is some expectation for you, which you must meet. JOSHUA 1vs6-9:BE STRONG AND OF A GOOD COURAGE:FOR UNTO THIS PEOPLE SHALT THOU DIVIDE FOR AN INHERITANCE THE LAND,WHICH I SWARE UNTO THEIR FATHERS TO GIVE THEM.ONLY BE THOU STRONG AND VERY COURAGEOUS ,THAT THOU MAYEST OBSERVE TO DO ACCORDING TO ALL THE LAW,WHICH MOSES MY SERVANT COMMANDED THEE:TURN NOT FROM IT TO THE RIGHT HAND OR TO THE LEFT,THAT THOU MAYEST PROSPER WHITHERSOEVER THOU GOEST.THIS BOOK OF THE LAW SHALL NOT DEPART OUT OF THY MOUTH ;BUT THOU SHALT MEDITATE THEREIN DAY AND NIGHT,THAT THOU MAYEST OBSERVE TO DO ACCORDING TO ALL THAT IS WRITTEN THEREIN:FOR THEN THOU SHALT MAKE THY WAY PROSPEROUS,AND THEN THOU SHALT HAVE GOOD SUCCESS.HAVE I NOT COMMANDED THEE? BE STRONG AND OF A GOOD COURAGE; BE NOT AFRAID, NEITHER BE THOU DISMAYED: FOR THE LORD THY GOD IS WITH THEE WHITHERSOEVER THOU GOEST.

This was now Joshua's turn to lead the Israelites into the Promised Land and GOD laid out what his character ought to be, if he were to make it. The same applies to us, we must be strong, bold, spiritually sound, be obedient to GOD, do as he commands. We must believe in our potential and speak to ourselves and to others positively, if we are to grow and produce and achieve what GOD has called us to be.

ISAIAH 48vs17: THUS SAITH THE LORD, THY REDEEMER, THE HOLY ONE OF ISRAEL; I AM THE LORD THY GOD WHICH TEACHETH THEE TO PROFIT, WHICH LEADETH THEE BY THE WAY THAT THOU SHOULDEST GO. It is GOD who opens doors of opportunities to grow, moving us from level one to level two. He teaches how to grow by means of ideas; concepts; principles; networks of people and opportunities to learn from others. Therefore our duty is to follow his teachings, and then only then can he lead us through the process of growth and help us make changes that are appropriate and GODLY, making profit/benefits along the way.

GROUP DISCUSSIONS

-If you are to compare and contrast your present circumstances and previous ones; let's say two years ago, can you honestly say you are happy with your growth or you are on target, and if yes; why and if not, why not?.

Are there areas in your life that you feel are hindering your comprehensive or total growth, If yes are you willing to confidentially share them with your Pastor or spiritual leader, and make an effort to change?.

Notes

_____

_____

_____

_____

_____

_____

_____

_____

_____

_____

_____

_____

_____

_____

_____

_____

THIRD PILLAR
TRUSTING GOD

Chapter Eight: We are not Alone

Life is a journey meant to be travelled with a purpose. No matter how you make your journey, the ultimate goal is to reach your destination. Not just getting there anyhow, but getting there as you have planned initially. That is achieving your goals amassing profits, using opportunities that present themselves to you, making wise decisions and shading off useless and irrelevant cargo.

"Circumstances we face everyday act as catalysts for the twists_and turns that define our journey."

Therefore then, there is need for support and counsel from others in order for us to accomplish that which we desire. Companionship therefore becomes pivotal in life. To have someone who you rely on is good. It makes the journey of life wholesome and complete and enjoyable. But as we move from one level to another in life we need to evaluate the friends and associates we attract or we get attracted to, with reference to their purposes in our lives and us in their lives as well. Some of my associates who are relevant today may not be relevant tomorrow, not because they would have done something wrong or bad, but I would have changed places in life, therefore I will need new or stronger support and knowledge to consolidate my new position in life.

"The desire for knowledge and security makes you to yearn for associates that are trustworthy".

Associates whose input in your life, you will understand and can use to achieve your goals. Understanding or full comprehension of someone or something is what builds my trust in that thing or person. This is how we as human beings ordinarily function.

GOD operates on mutual trust also .He is the author of trust. He knows what it can do in our lives, the motivation it brings, the support it renders, and the empowerment it builds in us. But as humans who are limited in our thinking we seem to put more of our trust in fellow humans and objects which are man-made than in the author of trust itself, GOD the Father. Even though we make lots of effort to trust GOD through our words and deeds, somehow we find ourselves more often than not, giving up on him and resorting to people. The number one reason for this is. People and their ways are easier for us to understand than GOD'S. We can comprehend each other's methods of operation and use them for our benefit.

Chapter Nine: Trusting up against Understanding

PROVERBS 3vs5: TRUST IN THE LORD WITH ALL THINE HEART; AND LEAN NOT UNTO THINE OWN UNDERSTANDING. Our desire to comprehend matters hinders us from fully relying on GOD.

<u>Trusting verses Understanding:</u> understanding seeks to supersede trusting. It is indeed logical that the more you understand something or someone, the more you trust that object or someone .The reverse is true, the less you understand the less you trust. Our understanding or comprehension acts then as a barometer of our trust in something or someone.

- For example the reason why we attend college, is to get understanding of whatever subject we choose to learn. No college/school or university can trust you by issuing their qualification, e.g.; a medical degree unless you prove to them first, that you understand medicine and its applications. You have to gain understanding first in order for the medical school to trust you with their certificates. If the medical school qualifies you, then all the people who trust that school will likewise trust you. The same applies with driving a car; you have to understand how an automobile (car) functions in order to operate/drive it. Then you can be trusted and be issued a driver's licence by the Traffic authorities.

- The same pattern applies with making financial investments. This is a critical area in one's life, so much thought and care is considered .Before you make your final decision about which bank or institute you are going to trust with your treasure, first you shop around, why ,because you want to understand

- the services offered, whether they suit into your plans and goals, -how credible the bank is, its assets value, scope of business, previous performances vision, management teams' qualifications , etc. In other words you want to understand its operations first before you can trust it with your business.

- In order for me to trust the food or medicine I take into my physical body I need to be knowledgeable about it first. When I visit a pharmacy/chemist for some medicine I notice that there is some information printed on the container of the medicine and this information includes:

-The manufacturer's name

-Name of the medicine

-Preservatives

-Dosage and directions for use

-Side effects and special precautions

-Storage instructions, etc.

All this is meant to inform me and make me understand this product, so that I trust it with my health.

This is how we get to trust each other;"Let me know you and know you fully well in order for me to trust you". This sequence of relationship building does not produce excellent results when it comes to our relationship with GOD. In GOD'S kingdom trust comes first, and then understanding will follow.

JOHN 2vs 1-11 :(Jesus' first miracle; the provision of wine at the wedding at Cana).

I believe what moved Jesus most than the need to provide wine at this wedding, was the degree of trust put on him by his mother and the servants that took instructions from him. It was the servant's first encounter with Jesus; they hadn't seen or heard about him before. They did not know him and yet they trusted him so much, that they took orders from him even though he wasn't their boss or bridegroom at this event. They were now working with Jesus because his mother had told them to. vs. 5: HIS MOTHER SAITH UNTO THE SERVANTS, WHATSOEVER HE SAITH UNTO YOU, DO IT. In other words she was saying I trust him and likewise you must trust him also. Jesus was not a winemaker by profession, his method or formula of making wine was sure enough to boggle the minds of these servants. He made them take water which was meant for something else, fill it to the brim into the water pots, not mixed with anything, and instantly serve it as wine. Now this defies logic, no normal right thinking human being can understand this. These guys did not understand what was going on or anyone for that matter would. Had they chose not to cooperate with Jesus because of his wine making method, surely their boss would have supported them. Yet they chose to cooperate with him, thus TRUSTING him, hoping that his method would ultimately produce the desired goal. That is the provision of the wine. So because of their cooperation and trust in the Lord everybody at the weeding later understood that indeed Jesus was the messiah. Therefore in order for us to experience the full provision, deliverance, support, protection and even healing in our lives we ought to trust him first. Even though we may not fully comprehend or understand his ways or methods of operation. What the word of GOD says we should do in order to have desired results: LETS DO IT. We must not seek to first understand, why and how the said method or principle works before we engage ourselves. Therefore when we have needs from the Lord and he calls us to cooperate, let's work with him, our cooperation simply benefits us in the end.

PSALM 107vs23-30:THEY THAT GO DOWN TO THE SEA IN SHIPS ,THAT DO BUSINESS IN GREAT WATERS;THESE SEE THE WORKS OF THE LORD ,AND HIS WONDERS IN THE DEEP. FOR HE COMMANDETH AND RAISETH THE STORMY WIND ,WHICH LIFTETH UP THE WAVES THEREOF.THEY MOUNT UP TO HEAVEN,THEY GO DOWN AGAIN TO THE DEPTH :THEIR SOUL IS MELTED BECAUSE OF TROUBLE.THEY REEL TO AND FRO,AND STAGGER LIKE A DRUNKEN MAN,AND ARE AT THEIR WIT'S END.THEN THEY CRY UNTO THE LORD IN THEIR TROUBLE AND HE BRINGETH THEM OUT OF THEIR DISTRESSES.HE MAKETH THE STORM A CALM,SO THAT THE WAVES THEREOF ARE STILL.THEN ARE THEY

GLAD BECAUSE THEY BE QUIET;SO HE BRINGETH THEM UNTO THEIR DESIRED HAVEN.

The word of GOD tells us about a people who entirely trusted GOD in their day to day business. People who dare to venture into projects that are very risky, where their lives are in danger, their skills are put to extreme tests, and their patience and inner strength is stretched beyond limit as well as their faith. In the midst of all these tests this group of people hangs on to their trust in the lord. What could be their secret we may ask? Well the secret lays in acknowledging the following 3 elements at their disposal:

1-GREAT WATERS (SEA); where they travel: business field

2-THE SHIP; which carries them in their travels/business

3-THE CAPTAIN OF THE SHIP; whose instruction they follow.

"The way or attitude you have in relating to the above 3 determines how and where you going to end up". Here is the explanation of this statement:

GREAT WATERS: This is your career, regardless of the training, experience you have in your field of occupation, the days are never the same. Each day brings forth its own challenges. Just like the great waters there are storms, rough seas, unfamiliar environmental conditions and overwhelming situations that confront us. Economic stabilities of our countries change, we lose our sources of income .What then do we do in such circumstances?

THE SHIP: This is the word of GOD. It is your carrier, it is strong enough to withstand the rough seas and yet light enough to suspend/sustain you over waters that may drown, weaken or even kill you. The word of GOD sustains you, protects and shields you, comforts, warms and houses you. It makes you distinct, you stand out can't be overlooked. It takes you places where ordinarily you would not be able to go. It promotes and advances you.

THE CAPTAIN: This is the Holy Spirit. He is the leader. He knows the direction we should take. He can foresee clearly the behaviour of the "seas". He knows what lies ahead better than anyone else. He calms you down; he assures you and desires that you succeed. He reveals the good and the bad to you. He takes care of your finances, health, and other socio-economic challenges if allowed to. He speaks to you, therefore you ought to listen and do as he says to show that you trust him.

IMAGINE WHAT WOULD HAPPEN IF YOU DO NOT LISTEN TO THE ADVICE OF THE **CAPTAIN** WHEN THE **SEAS/WATERS** ARE ROUGH AND YOU DECIDE THE **SHIP** IS NOT SAFE OR GOOD ENOUGH TO PROTECT YOU, AND YOU OPT TO JUMP AND SWIM TO SAFETY BY YOURSELF.

Trusting, relying and depending on GOD are not based on perpetual comfort. More often than not, GOD removes your comforts, securities to catapult you into another level of knowing his ways. Sometimes our experiences, education and achievements hinder us from the most wonderful relationship any human being can ever have, that is having strong trust in GOD.

Chapter Ten: To be Rooted

JOB 13vs15: THOUGH HE SLAYS ME, YET WILL I TRUST HIM: BUT I WILL MAINTAIN MINE OWN WAYS BEFORE HIM. Here is a man who once had everything anybody in his country would ever wish for. Job was not just rich in material things; he also had a family that knew how to take care of the blessings GOD had given them. He had responsible servants and children who valued and maintained unity in the family. The bible says so in chapter one of this book of Job. Before tragedy struck Job's trust in the lord was profound and the Lord was boastful of him. The Lord protected him all round so much that the devil knew about it and even said so to GOD. Now when GOD, because of Job's fear let Satan to mess with Job's life, it became unbearable for Job. He lost everything he had including his family in a very short period of time. You can imagine spending so much years building an empire for yourself only to lose it in no time at all. In such a situation anybody is bound to fight, get depressed, have a nervous breakdown, be filled with hate, bitterness and feel let down by GOD and probably walk away from him and anything to do with him. This was indeed a difficult time for Job. His wife, the helper from the Lord advised him to cut ties with GOD Because according to her The Lord had been very unfair to them.

But in the above scripture we read the words of a man who knew the root of all the wealth he had, this was a man who knew that as long as the root was intact and connected, life was worth fighting for. In spite of losing everything, his trust (the root) in GOD remained unwavering. It is this trust ,this link between him and The Lord that brought into his life a new beginning .During the turmoil Job's wife could not understand what was happening so did he, and his friends. Virtually everybody sought to search and understand the cause of this disaster, but nobody could.

"Your lack of understanding matters must not hinder you from trusting GOD".

When all hell breaks loose on you and you do not understand whats going on, it is fundamental that you increase your trust in The Lord. Get deeper and stronger as far as obeying him is concerned. Remember you have the word of GOD, the Holy Spirit and ability to communicate with The Lord (prayer), and his ministers at your disposal. Therefore when you lose your source of income I urge you to trust him. When you lose your loved ones, trust him. When you lose property/assets trust him. When your health is under test, trust him. When your integrity is under test, trust him. You need to have a firm belief in GOD'S ability to come through for you, when in situations that are beyond your comprehension.

JEREMIAH 17vs7-8: BLESSED IS THE MAN THAT TRUSTETH IN THE LORD, AND WHOSE HOPE THE LORD IS.FOR HE SHALL BE AS A TREE PLANTED BY THE WATERS, AND THAT SPREADETH OUT HER ROOTS BY THE RIVER, AND SHALL NOT SEE WHEN HEAT COMETH, BUT HER LEAF SHALL BE GREEN; AND SHALL NOT BE CAREFUL IN THE YEAR OF DROUGHT, NEITHER SHALL CEASE FROM YIELDING FRUIT. This scripture talks about a phenomenal blessing that follow those who trust the Lord. These are the people whose hope in the Lord is unwavering regardless of the difficult circumstances they might face. When we really trust the Lord, he injects inside us extraordinary resistance to the forces that otherwise would destroy us. What can take your neighbour down; will not take you down because you are like the above mentioned tree's leaves which defy the effect of heat, which normally would dry up every leaf of every tree within its reach. Even when you sense or foresee trouble or complications coming your way, choose not to pay too much attention to them. Why, because you know their effect on you will not stop the good, GOD has planned for your life. You do not quit your dream because those people who pledged to support you and your dream have suddenly decided to withhold their support, NO! You have the potential to produce fruit even in the midst of drought.

"You defy the odds and prove the critics wrong."

Why, because you trust The Lord and do not lean on your own understanding of issues.

PSALMS 37vs 3-5: TRUST IN THE LORD, AND DO GOOD; SO SHALT THOU DWELL IN THE LAND, AND VERILY THOU SHALT BE FED.DELIGHT THYSELF ALSO IN THE LORD: AND HE SHALL GIVE THEE THE DESIRES OF THINE HEART. COMMIT THY WAY UNTO THE LORD; TRUST ALSO IN HIM AND HE SHALL BRING IT TO PASS.

<u>GROUP DISCUSSIONS</u>

-Are there any times in your life, you regret for not trusting GOD enough and you wish you had known better to entirely put your trust in him. If any can you share the highlights with the rest of the group.

Why do you think, we often ignore the direction of the Holy Spirit and choose to do it our way even though we know we must be led by the Holy Spirit.

Notes

_____

_____

_____

_____

_____

_____

_____

_____

_____

_____

_____

_____

_____

_____

_____

_____

_____

FOURTH PILLAR
THE ABILITY IN YOU

Chapter Eleven: Release and manage

In an open cast mine, they use all sorts of heavy machinery to work. Some of the machines they use are those giant earth-moving machines commonly known as caterpillars. These machines are driven dip into the mine .They carry hundreds of tonnes of earth particles mixed with the minerals being mined, be it coal, gold, diamonds etc. When fully loaded they load these deposits into equally large and strong Tippers which then bring the deposits up to the earth's surface. A close look at these vehicles shows that these are no ordinary machines, they are massive in size. For example the diameter of a single tyre of a tipper- truck could be the average height of a basket ball player the weight thereof can be equal to a small automobile. All this and the rest of the machine are built with the type of work the machine is supposed to do in mind.

"The purpose is determined during the planning stage".

The manufacturer considers the characteristics of the cargo to be carried, the environment to be exposed to, the skills the operator must have, the expected number of years to work(life span),the degree of endurance ,all this and more is in cooperated during the designing and manufacturing stage. This is done in order to maximise the performance of the machine. This then points to the fact that no major changes should be done to the machine during its use, which should completely change its original design or purpose. If there be any enhancement, it should be in line with the original design. In other words, we can only work on improving the performance of what is there, not on the original design .The designing is the job of the manufacturer to worry about. The manufacturer and the operator share one goal though, that is to achieve maximum satisfactory results out of the machine.

The same is common to us humans, There has to be one goal between you (your spirit; the operator) and your creator, GOD (the manufacturer), that is to have satisfactory output from the machine (your body &soul). Everything that can make you live a fulfilling life is trapped inside you. All you need to do is release it and manage its performance. The talents, gifts, intelligence, wisdom inside us need proper management from us, not a complete overhaul. Overhauling is the work of the creator. Ours is to boost what we have, by means of trainings, fitness exercises, and making good life decisions on socio economic matters and so forth.

The reason why we need proper management of what GOD has freely given us is for us to maintain or increase the strength inside us. Remember that when you release or use some power, you need to make an inventory of whets left after use. This then leads to the question: How do you take stock of this strength and what and where can be the best source of this power be? Please note that strength is power in storage ready to be put to use when the need arises.

LUKE 4vs32: FOR THEY WERE ASTONISHED AT HIS DOCTRINE: FOR HIS WORD WAS WITH POWER. Our power is wrapped inside the word of GOD. The information we get in the word is our strength. Therefore when we start to use it we become powerful. It's all in there: the word of GOD. The amount of word in you is relational to the power you have or you can produce. Our Lord Jesus in chapter 4 of the book of Luke demonstrated the above in totality. First Jesus activated the power (in the word) when he faced the devil in the wilderness. Because of the strength (knowledge of the word) in him, Jesus was able to powerfully resist all the temptation the devil presented before him. For instance Jesus would use the phrase "it is written "meaning in this context "this is what I believe and live by".

"Therefore what you believe and live by; becomes your source of power."

My question to you is; what do you believe and what do you live by? JOHN 1vs 12:BUT AS MANY AS RECEIVED HIM.TO THEM GAVE HE POWER TO BECOME THE SONS OF GOD,EVEN TO THEM THAT BELIEVE ON HIS NAME.A simple answer can be found in the scripture above. If you believe that Jesus Christ is the son of the living GOD and accept him as your Lord and personal saviour and allow the word of GOD (the holy Bible) to mould and shape your life. Then you are setting yourself for some divine empowerment .You will be able to perceive, comprehend and achieve what ordinarily would be unachievable by a person of your status or background. The source of your would-be accomplishments is strong and sound. It can withstand any resistance coming to you, overcome any challenge thrown at you, and defeat any enemy against you. Therefore if you want to be triumphant always, believe and live by the word of GOD, accept it, and act on it without reservations.

The Apostle Paul puts it this way: ROMANS 1vs16: FOR I AM NOT ASHAMED OF THE GOSPEL OF CHRIST: FOR IT IS THE POWER OF GOD UNTO SALVATION TO EVERYONE THAT BELIEVETH: TO THE JEW FIRST, AND ALSO TO THE GREEK. Our power as the children of GOD is in the gospel, the spoken word, the preached word. This is the word that saves us and ultimately gives us the ability to be above circumstances that whether we like it or not, find their way into our lives on daily basis. And yes indeed, this is not shameful but worth sharing with others. We must realize that whatever we possess right now, all the material, physical accomplishments we have attained can disappear into thin air. We can lose everything we have worked for, in a snap of a moment, and never have it back, regardless of the insurance and assurance arrangements we might have in place. The only platform or ground we have that can bounce us back with a bang and eliminating all the negative feelings of the past: is the word of GOD. It is the only power that can propel us to much greater heights than before and be able to look back and say; we are glad we went through the initial lose in the first place. Why? The power in the word builds character; you are melted, refined and moulded gently, as well as being enlightened. Your glory will be replaced by another glory, thus moving from glory to glory or from an achievement to another.

Chapter Twelve: Phases of Action

The potential that has been invested in you by GOD is not meant for you to safe-keep or bank.

"You are not investors but spenders as far as your abilities are concerned".

By using what you got, you appreciate value. The more you seize opportunities to exercise what you know about a particular subject, the better you become in that field or subject. Practice makes perfect. You must also remember that, that which you are able to do as an individual must benefit not only you but others too. In fact it is your community, your family, your church, the organisation you work for, the college you attend your country and to a large extend the whole planet that must enjoy the benefits of your work more than yourself. This is what GOD had in mind when he made an investment in you.

DEUTERONOMY8vs17-18: AND THOU SAY IN THINE HEART, MY POWER AND THE MIGHT OF MINE HAND HATH GOTTEN ME THIS WEALTH, BUT THOU SHALT REMEMBER THE LORD THY GOD: FOR IT IS HE THAT GIVETH THEE POWER TO GET WEALTH. We need to know that it is not our education, networks or our family background etc that are the backbone of our well being. We are empowered by GOD initially in order to get into what we can physically depend on. Therefore my abilities are not founded on my education, career or who am acquainted with in human terms. I get attracted or connected to whoever I now know or whatever I possess because of the GOD –given power/ability that works in and through me. Therefore I must be conscious of this truth: it's not me but The Lord.

PHILIPPIANS 4vs13: I CAN DO ALL THINGS THROUGH CHRIST WHICH STRENGTHENETH ME: For as long as we are conscious of the above truth, we are set achieve a lot in our lives. We can have successful careers through Christ, we can have fruitful ministries through Christ, we can run profitable businesses through Christ, and we can build blessed families through Christ. Having this absolute knowledge strengthens us every day as we face different challenges that would otherwise overwhelm us.

EPHESIANS 6vs10: FINALLY, MY BRETHREN, BE STRONG IN THE LORD, AND IN THE POWER OF HIS MIGHT. Apostle Paul urges us to know what the word of GOD says about particular circumstances we might face, and not only that but also be able to apply the word in that particular circumstance. We must be able to move from knowledgeable people to being practical, that's from strong people to powerful people, from hearers to doers.

"Not all strong people are powerful people".

You might be strong and indeed display your strength but if you are not skilful in utilising your strength against your enemy then you are not powerful and **you won't win a battle.** Then you have no one to blame but yourself. How then do we move from being a strong people to a powerful people?

Chapter Thirteen: The Movement and its steps

Firstly we must understand that the information, knowledge we have about GOD and the words of Jesus Christ strengthens us. Secondly the works and character of Jesus Christ and actions of GOD empower us. In other words we are strong because we know the word of GOD and we are powerful because we apply the word of GOD appropriately.

MARK 9vs28-29: AND WHEN HE WAS COME INTO THE HOUSE, HIS DISCIPLES ASKED HIM PRIVATELY, WHY COULD NOT WE CAST HIM OUT? AND HE SAID UNTO THEM, THIS KIND CAN COME FORTH BY NOTHING, BUT BY PRAYER AND FASTING. Jesus Christ answers a question after his disciples failed to cast out a dump spirit out of a young boy. Jesus tells them to "fast and pray" in order to be powerful because LUKE 9vs43 records that the deliverance of this boy was a powerful act by Jesus. One of the reasons why we are told to fast during our programmes of prayer is because fasting helps us to focus on GOD and what we are praying for. Therefore then for us to be doers not hearers only, powerful and not strong only, people of action not people of information only, we must be a focused people. Below are 5 steps of application of the word I found out, help me to be person of influence in life.

*Step 1: **Admit** your limitations; show GOD that you have a problem and you need help. In EXODUS 4vs 10 Moses acknowledged that he could not speak or sound well before Pharaoh the king of Egypt. By admitting your limitations or weaknesses you are actually accepting the fact that whatever challenge that is before you, cannot be overcomed without the assistance of someone: you cannot by yourself make it.

*Step 2: **Listen** to what the word says about your limitations or situation. In JUDGES 6vs11-14, GOD speaks to Gideon when the children of Israel where under oppression of the Midianites. God directly addresses the situation Gideon is in. He mentions two things which are:

[1] "GOD is with you", because Gideon had been feeling abandoned by GOD because of the experiences he had been going through, even Israel as a nation.

[2] "Mighty man of valour" because Gideon was very disappointed by the powerlessness and hopelessness and cluelessness in the whole nation and how he could not do anything to change the circumstances of oppression. Therefore when GOD speaks to you, he specifically addresses your problem with a picture of who you are supposed to be.

"The picture, GOD has about me is what I am".

*Step 3: **Allow** the word to dwell inside you. David said he had hidden the word of GOD in his heart so that he would not sin against GOD. The physical heart is the engine of your life. The blood which gives your body life is pumped from there. The heart is not easily accessible it is protected all over by other parts of your body. So spiritually talking when you put the word of GOD in your spiritual heart, you are giving it uttermost importance and value, and circumstances that can weaken your faith will not easily have their way, because you know the truth and you have it in you. Know the word by heart.

*Step 4: **Permit** the word to your circumstance or situation in other words let the heart (which houses the word) pump out blood (the word) in order to live. 2KINGS 5 vs 10-14:AND ELISHA SENT A MESSENGER UNTO HIM,SAYING,GO AND WASH IN JORDAN SEVEN TIMES,AND THY FLESH SHALL COME AGAIN TO THEE,AND THOU SHALT BE CLEAN.BUT NAMMAN WAS WROTH,AND WENT AWAY,AND SAID,BEHOLD,I THOUGHT,HE WILL SURELY COME OUT TO ME, AND STAND,AND CALL ON THE NAME OF THE LORD HIS GOD,AND STRIKE HIS HAND OVER THE PLACE,AND RECOVER THE LEPER.ARE NOT ABANA AND PHARPAR,RIVERS OF DAMASCUS BETTER THAN ALL THE

WATERS OF ISRAEL?MAY I NOT WASH IN THEM,AND BE CLEAN?SO HE TURNED AND WENT AWAY IN A RAGE.AND HIS SERVANTS CAME NEAR,AND SPAKE UNTO HIM AND SAID,MY FATHER IF THE PROPHET HAD BID THEE DO SOME GREAT THING,WOULDEST THOU NOT HAVE DONE IT?HOW MUCH THEN ,WHEN HE SAITH TO THEE,WASH ,AND BE CLEAN?THEN HE WENT DOWN ,AND DIPPED HIMSELF SEVEN TIMES IN JORDAN,ACCORDING TO THE SAYING OF THE MAN OF GOD:AND HIS FLESH CAME AGAIN LIKE UNTO THE FLESH OF A LITTLE CHILD,AND HE WAS CLEAN. The above text of scripture reveals the following truth that we must know:

[1]Know that GOD works in ways that are beyond our human comprehension our methods are not necessarily his methods of doing things.

[2]Do not despise GOD'S methods of meeting your needs. Remember that GOD is your creator he knows all about you more than you do of yourself. His plans are not to harm you, no not at all.

[3]Do what is instructed. Our GOD is the GOD of order, when you follow his instructions, you make him smile and I suppose you know what that means when someone smiles at you.

*Step 5: **Acknowledge** that it is not you, but Christ Jesus (the anointed one and his anointing).ACTS 14vs 15a: AND SAYING, SIRS, WHY DO YE THESE THINGS? WE ALSO ARE MEN OF LIKE PASSIONS WITH YOU.....When Paul and Silas ministered to a man born crippled and he walked; the people who were present started to glorify them, equating them to their gods. But the Apostles forbid them right away by telling them that it was not them who had healed this man but GOD the almighty. And they reminded the onlookers that; they were as human as everybody who was there. They refused to accept the credit, the adoration, honour and glory brought upon them by the people who had seen the power of GOD. Instead they redirected the praise to our Lord Jesus Christ. This is what is going to keep you grounded or humble as you move from one breakthrough to another in your life.

Classification of the 5 steps

Steps 1; 2; 3 strengthen you; they establish you as person of a strong belief.

Steps 4; 5 empower you; they kick you into action and make you a vessel of honour which GOD can use without hesitation.

Mostly we are just strong and not powerful. We allow the word in our lives but do not permit it to work our lives. This is like allowing or giving someone the keys to your car in the garage but not permitting him/her to drive it, he/she gets into the car anytime he/she wants but cannot move it .Not because he/she does not want to drive it but you have not given the green light to use the car, for whatever reason you personally know.

My question to you is: are you not suffocating the will of GOD in your life? He wants to act or work, his hand (the Holy Spirit) is itching to get busy in you and through you. Let me close by a summary of my testimony. There was a time I desperately needed employment .I had no other choice but to get a good paying job because many plans concerning my wedding were on the ground. I realised and admitted that I needed GOD not people to help me. GOD through his word I heard preached at church and through my personal readings instructed me to seek him in prayer focussing on my need and I did that for 40 days. I meditated on what I read from the bible as I sought him, it did not matter whether I was in a bus or laying on my bed, I had to allow the word to dwell inside me. By doing that GOD gave meaning to the scriptures I read and I started to practise them, for instance I gave my offerings when he said so to me. This is what I believe gave the breakthrough of getting the job which came with fringe benefits of among other things the use of a company car and a company cell phone as well. When I started working it was not me alone who saw the goodness of the Lord but also those who were familiar with my situation, came along and we glorified GOD together. The details of this testimony I will never forget.

GROUP DISCUSSIONS

Can you confidently say that you are a strong Christian basing your fact on how much you know about the word of GOD and its potential to work in you? And discuss further giving one occasion you stood by the word and it produced the results in your life that made you a powerful Christian.

In your own opinion what are some of the habits we must be on the look out for that hinder us from moving, from being a strong people to a powerful people or from hearers only to doers, as the Lord expects us to be.

Notes

_____

_____

_____

_____

_____

_____

_____

_____

_____

_____

_____

_____

_____

_____

_____

FIFTH PILLAR
MUCH FRUIT

Chapter Fourteen: The Flash Points

When GOD created the earth, not only did he give life to it, he also gave fruitfulness to it. Inside all the plants, creatures that exist in this wonderful planet of ours, is the ability to bear fruit. It is because of fruitfulness that we can hope and plan for tomorrow. Our plans are based on the fact that, we are doing something today that we know or hope will bear fruit tomorrow. What we have today in our planet is a result of what the previous generations did to this planet. We are the fruits of the previous generations. How they behaved, conducted themselves, their values, mistakes, goals, expertise, experiments; all summed up produced this generation in its present state.

PSALMS 1vs 1-3: BLESSED IS THE MAN THAT WALKETH NOT IN THE COUNSEL OF THE UNGODLY, NOR STANDETH IN THE WAY OF SINNERS, NOR SITTETH IN THE SEAT OF THE SCORNFUL.BUT HIS DELIGHT IS IN THE LAW OF THE LORD; AND IN HIS LAW DOTH HE MEDITATE DAY AND NIGHT .AND HE SHALL BE LIKE A TREE PLANTED BY THE RIVERS OF WATER, THAT BRINGETH FORTH HIS FRUIT IN HIS SEASON: HIS LEAF ALSO SHALL NOT WITHER; AND WHATSOEVER HE DOETH SHALL PROSPER. In this scripture the psalmist mentions the conditions that are good for fruitfulness. There is an environment that helps breed good fruit and another that helps breed bad fruit.

1-STAY AWAY

The company or friends and the actions that you associate with are fundamental as far as productivity is concerned. For example if my friends are goal getters and hardworking, I will be inclined to think like so. I cannot help but start to set goals for myself and begin to work hard towards achieving them, thats if I still want to keep company with my pals. The reverse is true if my friends are lazy I'm inclined to go that route. The bible make it plain that those who do not honour the word of GOD, Its instructions and recommendations are not healthy associates as far as fruitfulness is concerned, they hinder you from producing good fruit. As such holiness and purity are fundamental elements of GODLY fruitfulness. Stay away from habitual transgressors of the will of GOD that is in the word. This is the first condition you have to meet in your pursuit of wholesome and good fruitfulness. God hates ungodliness, sin and scornfulness.

2-GO- AFTER

Desire the will of GOD, love to know it. Take comfort in what it says and be joyful about its effect in your life. Let it be the basis of your life decisions. In life there are moments when we have to make crucial decisions and make them quick. The immediate most reliable consultant we can contact and be sure that his advice is the right one, is the Holy Spirit. He will immediately speak to our inner person and remind us what the word says concerning that moment and directs us towards what we need to do, to be triumphant. It's important to have the word inside us because the Holy Spirit reminds us of what we have deposited in our hearts. If our hearts do not have the word, the Holy Spirit has nothing to remind us of, thereby leaving us with no GODLY strategy. I urge you to enjoy going after or pursuing the will of the Lord, that is wrapped in the word of GOD. Ask the Holy Spirit he is always willing to help; after all he is our helper, and our comforter.

3-STAY WITHIN

As I mentioned before, you must stay in an environment that will flourish you. One observation I have made, which I know you must have, also, is that for tomatoes to maintain their freshness flavour or taste and even colour and attractiveness, you need to keep them in a cold environment such as a refrigerator. If you do so, you are sure to have them in a good state for a long time. So it is the cold conditions that can make the tomatoes maintain their freshness. It is therefore very crucial to keep yourself within or maintain companionship of people who through the word of GOD, advise you, encourage you, motivate you and positively criticise you.

Chapter Fifteen: Principal Seasons and fruits

In verse 3 of the scripture mentioned earlier, it is said that a tree produces fruit in its season. Seasons are times we are in. There is never a moment you are not in a season. If it's not summer, it could be autumn or winter or spring. Therefore if your best season is not winter do not lose hope, hang on spring could be the time you flourish. And if you flourish in spring then spring becomes your season of fruitfulness.

The same verse talks about being planted by the rivers of water: Please Note; it is the tree that is by the rivers of water not the rivers of water that are by the tree. It is the circumstances that have you not vice versa. For example if get sick, it is sickness that has you not you having a sickness, because no one in his /her right mind would want to be sick. In reference to the tree again, the tree was PLANTED, it did not choose its location, but GOD did. More often you are controlled, than you control. As people who are still alive, we function in 3 different areas of existence which are:

FAMILY: we are members of a physical family, we belong to a certain household, we are born in a certain family and we are moulded by the culture of that particular family.

CAREER: we are earning our living by doing something .We have jobs which we do professionally or otherwise.

MINSTRY: we are expected to do what GOD wants as far as his kingdom is concerned. He has put in us different attributes to be used to enlarge his kingdom here on earth, whether we know it, like it or don't.

The 3 seasons if you like; have us, we do not have them. My family have me as a son .I am born therein and did not choose to be a member. My career has me also; the financial factors that affect my industry affect me in a way. If there is a slow down economically in my profession naturally I feel the effects, regardless of what I may wish for, to happen, somehow I am controlled by the economic factors. My ministry is the work of the Lord through me, it is GOD in action using my physical being and his blessing on top of it all. Therefore it is him not me as such we are framed by our families, careers and ministries. In all these "frames" or "seasons "we are to bear fruit, because we are fed from the rivers of water: the word of GOD...Please Note: These seasons run concurrently therefore wisdom to strike a balance is needed.

FAMILY SEASON:

For every family to function harmoniously there has to be **unity**. The members of the family must understand that they are one, In spite of the differences that may occur in terms of opinion, education, wealth, beliefs etc. But unity is not easy to achieve, it is not delivered on a silver platter. We have to work hard to achieve it. As a member of a family who is geared for fruitfulness you ought to make the production of unity in the family a major fruit you have to bear among other wishes you might have for your family. You must understand that in a family we carry each other's burdens and we share our losses and successes. When one member of the family is in trouble, it means also you're in trouble and it's your duty to help him/her to come out of it. The same applies with success, when you're successful, your success is not just for you alone, but must be shared with the whole family. The onus is upon you to protect the family, whether it's the immediate or extended family. This you can do by praying for it, offering material, socio-economic support to the members whenever the need arises. Remember you are expected to love regardless of the shameful behaviour some members of the family might bring upon the family. Probably the only action that will make them change is your love towards them and continuously showing them that you are a united family and will thrive to remain such, no matter the circumstances.

Age is of paramount importance in trying to maintain unity in the family. You must know that there are elders and they deserve respect that is due to them. You might be more financially sound than them, still this does not erase the fact that the elderly have more experience about life than you, and their word deserve careful consideration in family matters. The same applies to those younger than you. Consider their opinions and advise accordingly making it clear to them that you wish them prosperity and a good future and that they can always approach you with their fears, confusion and mistakes and indecisions. You must also acknowledge that there are some areas in life ,other family members are more gifted or better equipped in that you ,and as such those members deserve to be given room to function in those areas ,should the need arise.

"Constructive criticism is healthy in a family; it keeps our attitudes and egos in check."

Admitting our failures and be willing to accept help bonds the family.

CAREER SEASON:

I strongly believe that there is no career or profession or job that is independent of other careers. Our professions are intertwined. We need each other to function successfully. A salesperson needs a manufacturer of a product and a consumer to realise profit in his/her career. A medical doctor needs a supplier of medicines and equipment and a patient to release profit in his/her career. Therefore the desire to make profit is what drives our careers. Profit can be and not limited to finances, gaining more knowledge is profit; in a nutshell a positive addition to whatever you possess or know right now is profit. As such **profit** is a fruit worthy producing during the course of your career. ISAIAH 48vs17: THUS SAITH THE LORD, THY REDEEMER, THE HOLY ONE OF ISRAEL: I AM THE LORD THY GOD WHICH TEACHETH THEE TO PROFIT, WHICH LEADETH THEE BY THE WAY THAT THOU SHOULDEST GO. In whatever profession you are in, know that you are not the first in there. Others before you have practised it. They may not have shared the same experience you are having but it is advisable to always refer to their experiences, you might pick-up one or two helpful insights. No matter how skilled you might be, remember that you are just as human as the least skilled person next to you. Your professional achievements do not give you the right to scorn other people. The unskilled have 5 senses just like you, they can smell, taste, touch, hear, and see. Because the global economic climate changes; the demand of your field of training is not guaranteed to last forever, therefore make the most of it right now. Be as productive as you can possibly be, because your skills may not be needed tomorrow, respecting others' views on matters of work experience is encouraged.

Develop a habit of listening and observing and followed by thinking and acting. In this way you develop your learning skills and leadership qualities. Observing is important because it brings reality before your eyes. Then you can now start to plot how to deal with the situation before you. Every environment has rules and regulations that govern it, that must be observed. You ought to conduct yourself accordingly if you want to stay in the game. For example in an establishment there are timetables to start work and to knock off; stick to them if you still want your job. Share information with others less fortunate. Not everyone knows what you know and many may wish they did. Therefore share tips of the trade with others, train others if called to. If you are an employee it is a blessing to wish your employer or boss well in every area of his/her life. Do unto others as you would want them do unto you. Treat the organisation you are involved with as your own, desire that it prospers, grow and make profit. Lastly never forget that GOD has you in your field for a good reason, he has good thoughts towards you, to make you success.

MINISTRY SEASON:

When Jesus was about to leave for heaven, he ordered the disciples to go into the whole world and preach the gospel; the good news to every person. He ordered them to do so because he wanted **multiplication** to take place in the kingdom of GOD. The people who had accepted him as the messiah, the saviour of the whole world needed to be increased in number. The kingdom of GOD is not meant for a small group of people but for the whole world irrespective of ethnicity, race or creed. Therefore multiplication became and still is the vision for preaching the gospel. Whether your ministry is in music, teaching ,administration, media etc, the degree of increase of influence in what you do reflects on whether you are expanding the kingdom or not.

As a minister you must acknowledge that you take orders from a higher authority. It is the will of the Lord that must be done, not yours, no matter the circumstances might be. Holiness is paramount, our GOD is holy so must we be. Sin must be dealt with immediately and without hesitation. Our GOD is faithful and just, to forgive us. Where sin is entertained ,the presents of GOD departs.1 CORINTHIANS 16vs9:FOR A GREAT DOOR AND EFFECTUAL IS OPENED UNTO ME,AND THERE ARE MANY ADVERSARIES.GOD does open doors of opportunities for you, if you choose to get involved with his work. These opportunities are for the advancement of his kingdom. As these opportunities come, so does the devil, to block us from taking these opportunities. He does this in many different ways, such as bringing disharmony in the church, family and workplaces. Delaying tactics which will breed impatience and an unstable heart which will make us lose focus, and most of the time fear and timidity resulting in us not moving forward into what we know GOD has said we should do. Factors such as these suffocate progress in our lives and we should guard against them.

We need to be a people who communicate often with our father GOD. Let's talk to him, because he loves to talk with us. Tell him all, I mean everything about the whole circumstances. A praying person is a powerful person, whom GOD will use to do powerful things on earth. Reading the word of GOD is not enough, let's study it. The Holy Spirit reveals the truths of the kingdom to those who study the word. He shows them what to do in their ministries, he maps the way, even when it seems there is no way forward. We must honour the Holy Spirit; he is what GOD has given us here to operate in and with. Do you need some profound revelations, divine favours, and breakthroughs after breakthroughs, wisdom and guidance, then respect the Holy Ghost, give him space in your ministry.1 JOHN 4vs21: AND THIS COMMANDMENT HAVE WE FROM HIM, THAT HE WHO LOVETH GOD LOVE HIS BROTHER ALSO. If we claim that we love the Lord, then we must love people also. The Lord Jesus came for the salvation of people and he ministered to people and died for people and rose again for the people and is seated at the right-hand side of the father interceding for the people, who have accepted him as the lord and saviour of their lives. He will come back for such a people. Therefore ministry is not about me or you, per say but about and for GOD and his people.

"Let's love GOD and his people"

You cannot operate in isolation, you need others. Get connected to other ministers who operate in the ministry such as yours. If you are a musician network with other musicians, share experiences, testimonies, by doing so you are strengthening others. PROVERBS 27vs17: IRON SHARPENETH IRON; SO A MAN SHARPENETH THE COUNTENANCE OF HIS FRIEND. What remains a challenge to you right now may be a challenge overcome by another. It is advisable to know how he/she overcomed it. It is indeed comforting just to know that I am not alone in this journey, there are others who are at the same level I am if not higher or lower. And are probably going through what I am experiencing as well. Better still we can share all this and more and pray for each other and bless each other as well.

GOD resists the proud and gives grace to the humble. If we want to affect positively our communities through the ministries we have, and then pride must be resisted outright because as our ministries grow so does the temptation to glorify ourselves as the best in that specific ministry, increase. But GOD does not allow any temptation that we cannot overcome, to come our way. Therefore we have the capacity to overcome pride and replace it with humility.

Please note we produce after our own kind, be it in the family, career or ministry .What is inside me is what I give birth to. If kindness is in me, kindness shall I produce .If intolerance is inside, so intolerance will I let out. The fruit we produce is primarily for others to enjoy. Selfishness has no room in the production of the kingdom of GOD'S fruit. Be consistent do not waiver, you will bear good fruit which can bring forth multiplication and enlargement in what you do. For example a well looked after orange tree produces an orange and inside that orange there are seeds that can produce many oranges.

CONSISTANCE======FRUITFULLNESS=======MULTIPLICAT ION

<u>GROUP DISCUSSIONS</u>

-How are you doing fruit wise in your family; career and ministry and what kind of fruit are you producing in each frame; is it a poor, good, excellent fruit .

-What could be your greatest challenge to fruitfulness?

Notes

LAST WORD

It is my wish that you excel in whatever you have set yourself to do. In spite of the seemingly huge obstacles before you, know that with a right attitude and positive frame of mind you can make it. Always remind yourself why you are pursuing that dream. Everything that surrounds you is meant for you to either learn from it or use it or support it or care for it or enjoy it or avoid it because it could derail you. As such divine wisdom from the LORD is very vital in order to make it.

GOD RICHLY BLESS YOU